Words Of Us

Christopher Klune

BookLeaf
Publishing

Presentation by *BookLeaf Publishing*

Web: www.bookleafpub.com

E-mail: info@bookleafpub.com

ISBN: 9789357696029

First edition 2022

To you, my sunshine

ACKNOWLEDGEMENT

To those that I have never thanked for giving me the courage to write.

TO THE MOON

1

Struggling to give
what meets the worth
Of years long journeys
in itself a gift, our stories
Laying mind bare
For you, of us

A NIGHT OUT

2

A story with two memories
One of swirling dust and country
Mutual smiles as
words cut through the noise
Stumbling back together
A swell of intimacy
A first night of many

DIM SUM

3

Dim Sum is love
or a gateway to it
In the coyness
The warm steam
dissolving icy eyes
An invitation
for early gifts

LAUGHING

4

My love has several
First is the flat, sarcastic sting
Second is the mocking kind, paired with a roll of
the eyes
Third is the awkwardly tinged genuine one,
nerves abound
Fourth is the low rounded one, shared with close
friends
Fifth is the one that hurts her stomach, used for
family
Sixth is the high, vibrant giggle paired with a
wide smile, pure bliss
Music to my ears

TIME

5

Words short
to describe feeling
a new world
within the old
Made by us
in short days and thick snow
Wandering, together
Letting go that inner child
exploring the world
again
Nothing
but fleeting time
together

AN EXPLOSION

6

The dangers of becoming comfortable
vulnerable to careless moments
To crystalize or disintegrate
The foundations of a bond
Mine moment was an explosion
Not of anger or affection, but nature
That fortunately, was met by wide-eyed laughter

SOMETHING LOST

7

She has her favorites and I have mine
An ode to a thought lost something
That was with you the whole time
As night blended with morning
Treasured words did chime

DOUBT

8

It's human to doubt
But you must know, your
Shape beautiful
Soul fierce
Mind curious
Presence comforting
Food soothing
Ambitions worthy
Humour inducing
Love unwavering
When shadows cast by doubt
Remember that warmth
that you walk in

LEAVING

9

Over oceans
Learning of love
and struggle
I remember
The night before
holding, until sore
So that my muscles remember
always

ELEVATOR

I knew it was special
when I was in an elevator
A short return
The last few hours, a cold winter night
Prolonging the goodbye at your door
I walk down the hall
Waiting for an elevator
I see you peek, and skip to me
A kiss, an embrace
Then, alone
in a cold metal box
holding back
these sorrowed circles

DISTANCE

Miles have been our teacher
through lessons of compassion and hurt
Heads wrapped around, wary
though it be through ocean or desert
and escapades that near, though apart
Thoughts of distance scary, though learned
with part of you, my heart

FLOWERS IN THE WIND

12

I remember when your mother
saw petals floating by
around cascaded mountains
"Hermosa"
Smiling to myself, thinking it normal
Little did I appreciate
eyes that shade anew, to make life again
A quality passed to you

TUGLUKTUK

13

I always thought my jokes were stupid
But enough to amuse me
Like when I say I am from Tugluktuk
A grin ear to ear
How amazing it is
To have someone by your side
Who laughs at them
…sometimes

COOKING

14

Something shared
Something given
Adoration from inside
Flavoured smiles with stories
many are those evenings
blurred and forgotten
but no less important
and not lost at all

QUIET

15

Afford me space for understanding
That in parts of joined anatomy
our quiet speaks volumes
when enveloped in a silence
not awkward nor agitated
that soothes nerves to sleep
Is a divine comfort
a rarity to keep

SOUNDS

All the sounds of us
Dazy evening laughter
Whispering embraces
Deafening silences
Eruptions of focused rage
Passionate infernos
Pattering of handheld footsteps
Gentle nighttime sways
Late morning rumblings
Soft pecks of affection
Tender healing apologies
Close quartered heartbeats
If quiet is vital to anatomy
So to sound should be
In encompassing vitality

PAIN

17

Realizing my learning too slow
Confronting a sense of self
Gripping, spiraling down a hole
Begging parts of you rebel
Stirring solely, in a ceaseless unknown

RENEWAL

18

Realizing a tender patience
Confronting a self destruction
Gripping, mounting the complacence
Begging myself reconstruction
Stirring together, each creating our essence

ROADS

19

Black pavement and time
make for moments
silly games and sleep
sun beaming down
from seeing writing on stone
to westward peaks
small towns of nothingness
plains that eyes cannot reach
in drive-thrus and borders
hands linked in seat
the hum of smokey metal machine
a place of temporal serene

COLOMBIA

This one is for a distant time away
imagined by family and sunsets
in small towns with long revelations
with cities blanketed by rhythm
among the origins of magic
with warmed ajiaco
and those fresh arepas
that only a mother can make
coffee filled mornings
that keep us awake at night
dancing to words and music
Eager to tell this story
a dream, therapeutic

AND BACK

Human blessings
are stories
I am privileged to
have many
Alone and not
People near and far
Across worlds and histories
But

The moments that weave
the stories
And those of will
To listen
Feed the sacred blessing
I suppose then I am blessed
For moments and ears
But

Poetry fails me
To describe, still
The persistent grace of
your presence
For in the multitude of stories
That encompass human condition
The most relieving constant

Is that someone to share
everything
Even
To the moon
and back